You
the
Graduate

Harold J. Drown

Abingdon Press
Nashville and New York

*Library of Congress cataloging in
Publication Data*

DROWN, HAROLD J. You the graduate
1. Success 2. Conduct of Life. I. Title.
BJ1611. D75   248'.42   73-18380

ISBN 0-687-46856-6

MANUFACTURED BY THE PARTHENON PRESS AT
NASHVILLE, TENNESSEE, UNITED STATES OF AMERICA

At graduation time an open door is before you, a door no one but you can shut. It is the door of success, and it leads to a life of advancement and achievement, a full and good life.

I admire people who strike out for themselves with ideas and ideals on the high side. I believe most of us miss out on life's greatest gift, the open door of success, by being either too afraid or too lazy to walk through it to tackle the problems that lie on the other side, to try for some new mountain top, or to run the risk of failure.

Life lies before you, the graduate. As you accept its invitation, promising to give your best, door after door will open.

To
our Grandchildren
James,
Elizabeth,
and
Janet Wile

An important requirement for successful living is to know that life is good. Then that belief must be lived to the full.

The world is so full of people who believe in a lot of things a little bit, but not in anything very much. And anyone who does not believe in something wholeheartedly has no goals, no ideals, and no future. But the person who believes in something good with all his heart and might is on his way—and will enjoy the trip.

Here is a thought worth holding on to. *Life is good.* Of course there are troubles, sorrows, and pains. No one escapes these. But life has a greater number of successes, happinesses, and gains. So in whatever condition you find yourself, start counting the blessings that are an abundant part of your life.

We have to believe in something, and we have to have faith in something. Otherwise life isn't worth living. So, let's look at these two great powers.

Belief is the foundation upon which we stand and build. The things, institutions, and people in which we believe form the background of life for all of us. They are factual and provable. But faith! Though we use the words interchangeably, faith runs on ahead of belief. It is the power that drives us toward an idea we have no proof of but would like to develop. In curbstone language, faith is the guts to risk something valuable in pursuit of an idea we can't prove. This is what gives zest to life, makes astounding discoveries, and creates impossible achievements—a powerful faith grounded in an immovable belief. Know what you believe about your God, yourself, and your world. Put your facts on paper. This is the foundation you will build your future upon.

Then, moving toward the dream side, what is your wildest ambition? Don't ask is it provable, but is it a great idea worth spending a lifetime to develop? Don't fool with anything less. You've got only one life, a short one. Don't waste it on the insignificant, but take the step in the dark toward some great goal and never give up. And be assured that the driving power of that faith will open doors that won't open to any other power.

You are a very unusual person. No one can stand where you stand, know what you know, feel what you feel, be what you are, or do what you do. Think of that for a moment. No one can do, be, feel, know, or think exactly as you can. That makes each one of us a very unusual person. The highest honor that could be bestowed has been granted to each of us, the honor of being a special person without a duplicate. Even identical twins are not completely identical. Man was not built by chain production methods. And this exclusiveness makes each of us very important to the whole scheme of humanity and eternity. God created nothing unimportant, and man is the chief glory of all His creation.

Believing this takes the competition out of life—with one exception. Man is always and forever to be in competition, not with his fellows, but with his own yesterdays. If any man will see to it that today he rises above yesterday in knowledge, in effort, in creating, in helpfulness, he will find a peace and a satisfaction that no competition with his neighbor could ever produce.

Now that you've graduated, your mind is filled with facts, ideas, and plans. But how about your face? How is that educated? You may not be able to change the shape of it, but you sure can change the look of it. And that look is a pretty good indication of the spirit that lies behind it. Check up on the people you know well. Their known faces match their known dispositions.

I want to give you a personal illustration that taught me something important. I was riding down on the elevator in a department store in Rochester, New York. A lady got out ahead of me and waited. As I left the elevator she said to me, "You're happy, aren't you?" I was somewhat taken aback by the unexpected statement. I answered, "I suppose so. I hadn't thought about it." She said, "It shows on your face, and I needed that this morning. Thank you." She turned and walked away. I had never seen her before, nor have I since. And I have no idea why I happened to have whatever look it was she caught on my face. But the incident told me that we even influence the lives of passers-by with the expressions we carry around on our faces.

But more than that. It is impossible to put a pleasant look on your face and keep it there very long without your spirits rising to match it. It is a bit of self-administered therapy that doesn't cost a penny and pays handsome dividends.

Almost everyone has heard the biblical story of the talents. One man had ten talents. He used them well and received ten more. One had five talents. He used his well and gained five more. But another man had only one talent, and he—being jealous of those who had more—refused to use his talent at all, and as a result he lost even that one.

The moral of this story is: It takes only one talent well managed to make a very successful and happy life. And no one was ever born without at least one talent. So many of us keep checking on the other fellow's abilities and opportunities, wishing they were our own. By spending our time and thoughts in this manner, we neglect to develop our own abilities and opportunities and then wonder why we are unhappy.

What talents others have is none of your business. If you live to the best of your ability, you have as good a chance of being successful as those who start off with more.

Every person ought to plan a few minutes each day when he can be by himself, a time when there are no distractions to take his mind from the very important business of examining himself, checking up on his direction, his aims and ambitions in life, reviewing his yesterdays, and planning for his tomorrows. When a person is alone, he doesn't try to fool himself about anything. He sees himself for just what he is. This is why some people can't stand to be alone; they don't like what they see.

But time spent alone pays dividends. If you have been meeting life and meeting it fairly, if you have given it your best, then these times alone will be rewarding, times for pleasant memories, times to review the past and to feel good about it.

But if you have not been playing fair, if you have been giving life less than your best, then time will rest uncomfortably and will give you an opportunity to get straightened out. Just fifteen minutes alone every day is a good prescription for happiness.

Do you want to be great? Sure you do. You should. It is one of your inalienable rights. So here is the formula.

1) Take stock of yourself. What do you like to do? What are your natural talents? Beat the bushes of your mind until you can answer that.
2) Go after every scrap of education available in the area of your interests.
3) Go to work full time and turn the clock to the wall.
4) Turn your attention to the Eternal now and then, with words like, "Open the way, Lord, and thank you." I'll lay you dollars to doughnuts he will do just that.
5) Never doubt your success, and let that certainty show in your face. Funny thing how success goes tumbling after the look of success.

The trouble with most of us is that we are always trying shortcuts. We leave out or give little attention to one or two of the steps in the formula. But know this for sure: Anyone who follows the above five in earnest will not fail but will make a great contribution to the world. What more can you ask out of one life?

Can we live and do all right without bothering with the Bible? Yes, of course we can. Many people do. Then why not? Because life isn't to be lived just "all right." The chance to get by in this life and even to do well without acknowledging God or his Word is one of the evidences of a God of great patience and mercy. He refuses to force people into line by threatening disaster upon them, and he refues to use as bait, "Be good and I'll pay you well."

The Bible is a textbook with illustrations telling and showing us how to take an all-right life and stretch it into a magnificent life.

If you read an understandable chapter from the Bible every day for three months, and attend church every Sunday during that three months, and if you deliberately put your mind to that reading and to the meaning of the service of worship, you will know the reason for the Bible and for the church. You will be on the way toward something more than an all-right life.

Life seems to be so constructed that there is a right time to do everything. And if we hurry things before their time, we are going to wind up unhappy and have to pay painful costs.

Recently, I was called to a home that was on the verge of breaking up. The boy was twenty, the girl nineteen, and their baby one month. Both parents had quit college. They were so very sure that their great love could stand any strain.

But now she couldn't go to work because of the baby, and he couldn't find work because of an inadequate education. These two young people had locked themselves in the type of prison into which so many young couples have hurried to outwit the time schedule.

It is right to leave school, but not before we have something to offer the world. It is right to marry and have children, but not before we are ready to take over the responsibilities of supporting a family. This couple had acted out of the time schedule and now too-heavy costs were rolling in.

Make the church a part of your life. It is for people who are not perfect, people like you and me. Most of us are there because we need help in meeting the temptations that line our daily avenues of life. A service of worship is a time for us to take a good look deep within ourselves and then to reach out in prayer (which is thinking on the highest level) for the help we need to overcome our weaknesses and fears.

The church may be likened to the dressing room of a great theater. Here is where we put on the garments and find the props that are needed out on the stage of life. Here is where we are prepared and cued for the next act.

At frequent intervals enter the church of your choice just to sit in those meaningful surroundings and think about the blessings that are yours, blessings you didn't earn, and maybe don't deserve; to think about how you came to be and why; to measure your life and the way you live against the lives of those great people who struggled and won; and to measure your behavior pattern against the commandments of God.

As we grow older and pass our milestones—and you have passed an important one here at graduation time—more and greater responsibilities crowd in upon us. Perhaps the biggest mistake we can make is to try to duck them. Unfortunately, when we think of responsibility we frequently think of something irksome, some unpleasant duty, some price to pay. But that is not at all true. Our responsibilities are the shells in which our opportunities come wrapped. Check this out: Those who complain about and try to duck as many responsibilities as they can are the same ones who complain about not getting the breaks. These breaks of life seem to follow on the heels of accepted responsibilities.

Do you know what the word "responsibility" really means? Just turn it around. Every responsibility accepted is evidence of your *ability to respond* to some invitation up the ladder. You can thank the good Lord that you have this *response-ability*. Suppose you couldn't respond to the calls of the needs around your. Suppose you didn't have the ability to say, "Sure I'll do it." If that were true, you would be a disappointment to yourself and a drag on society. But, by believing in yourself and having faith in the future, you will respond to the calls for your abilities, be glad you have them, and thus, rung by rung, climb higher and higher.

How often we hear, "I've worked hard all day. Now I want some fun." That's not a bad idea at all, but it seems to tell us that the day's work has been a tiresome chore and had no pleasure in it. And that is wrong, very wrong. We spend the greatest number of our waking hours at our work, and I refuse to believe that the idea of work was created as a punishment. Perhaps this happens because when some people start out in life, they take the first job that comes along just to be getting an income, or they take the best-paying job regardless of whether they like it or are fitted for it. And thus begins a lifetime of drudgery. When these people retire, they don't know how to enjoy their leisure because they never learned to enjoy their work.

Take a little time, if you possibly can, to look around for the kind of work that fits you and that you can find fun in doing. To have a happy life you must have a happy job. The purpose of work is to fulfill your need for development in body, mind, and spirit. Do that, and the pleasure in your work will pay big dividends.

Know thyself" is almost a cliché. And to discover ourselves is probably one of the most painful, and at the same time one of the most valuable, experiences in life. Too many of us simply refuse to recognize that there are areas in our lives that could do with a bit of changing. We like ourselves pretty well as we are. And that liking erects a blockade to further growth. We unconsciously train ourselves to overlook our weaknesses, to adjust to them by excuses or maybe by blaming somebody else. We resent being told what our shortcomings are. It takes a big person to check on himself and a still bigger one to profit by the criticism of others.

Criticism is something no one likes to have aimed at him. We are willing to admit we are not perfect, but we resent it when anyone tells us in what ways we are imperfect. In short, we resent criticism.

How should you react to criticism? First, ask if it is true. Be honest about that. If it isn't true, forget it. But if it is true, then start the machinery of change. It is a great satisfaction to change something in your life that you know should be changed.

One thing you should be willing to protect with every effort possible is your good name. The Bible says that a good name is worth more than great riches. Certainly that has been proved true. Al Capone became a very wealthy man, but his wealth had come from all the undercover, illegal rackets that destroy men, And so the name Al Capone became despised by decent men everywhere.

When your name is spoken, what does it mean to others? If you have cheated, lied, stolen, then that is what your name will mean to them. If you have been honest, friendly, cheerful, and a good sport, then you have brought honor to your name, and you have honored your parents who gave you that name.

Many people are unhappy because they don't complete anything. They fritter away their time on nonessentials. They keep busy, but at the close of the day they have very little of value to show for the hours spent. These people are restless, dissatisfied, and unhappy. They have missed the thrill of completing something.

These people may be called someday people. They are always going to do something someday. Any day now, they expect to get started on a magnificent project. But somehow that someday never materializes. This couplet by an unknown writer speaks to the point.

> Delay not 'til tomorrow to be wise;
> Tomorrow's sun to thee may never rise.

If each of us would start out today on the project we intend to do someday and make commendable progress toward the completion of it, we would have a world of great people doing great things. And the level of happiness would be on the rise.

Prayer is not magic. It is simply the way God made the world. Some things have to be dug for. Some things have to be waited for. Some things have to be called for. Some things have to be worked for. But there are still other things—very vital things —that have to be prayed for. These lie behind the locked door of life's safety deposit box. And these are available only to those who go after them with the key of prayer.

You may stand before your safety deposit box at the bank and shout at it. You may kick it and pound on it, even beg the bank attendant to open it. But that door to the values and riches that are already yours will not budge until you insert your key along with the attendant's in the lock.

Many of the highest values and greatest riches of this life lie behind the door to the Great Vault that will open only when you insert your key of prayer.

The good life and the happy life go hand in hand. I would like to quote something from a Roman poet named Martial. "To have lived so as to look back with pleasure on your past life is to live twice."

Each of us is continually filling his own picture gallery with memories. Every day we paint and hang a few pictures of what we did and said. And these are the pictures we have to look at. We control the happiness or the unhappiness of our own later years by the pictures we hang in our art gallery of memories.

No day is a thing in itself, having a beginning and an ending and then passing out of existence. But each day has a floor made of all the days that went before it, and each day is part of every day that follows.

If anyone really wants to be happy, he has got to give up a very cherished possession. He has got to give up the idea of "me first." He has got to stop looking at everything and everybody with an eye to what is there in this for me? The greatest Man who ever lived said it this way. "He that saves his life shall lose it, but he that loses his life shall find it."

What does this mean in our day and language? It means that one who spends the majority of time and talent making a bid for attention, advancing himself only and with no thought for the other fellow, will never find happiness. That person is too self-centered. This becomes evident to others very quickly, and they turn away.

But one who takes care of his own needs and at the same time lends a helping hand to others is guaranteed happiness.

It is good to know that the way of life as it is supposed to be lived is all set up. I hope you can believe this because it will make all the difference in the world to your sense of well-being. Life is no trial-and-error business. You may change your way of living, but no one changes the way life is supposed to be lived. Life is not your plaything, and the world is not your oyster. But life is your workshop fully equipped with all the tools, the raw ma-materials, and the blueprints you will ever need. Your tools are your talents. The raw materials are yourself, your fellow human beings, and all that nature produces. The blueprints are the history of those who have gone before, your own experiences, the Bible, and prayer.

With these you can walk confidently through life knowing that you do not have to establish your route, that you do not find your way only by the trial-and-error method, but that all you need do is follow the signs that are there to see if you will look and believe.

Do you sometimes feel that life hasn't been fair to you? Have you felt that others have had a much better break? All of us have allowed ourselves this excursion into self-pity. But what is fair? Do we mean by fair an equal distribution of wealth? What a stagnating condition that would be. Do we mean by fair that no one shall have more trouble than another? What placid-faced stoics we would become. Do we mean by fair that we should all be equally happy? What spineless personalities we would develop. Do we mean by fair that no one should be more popular than another? If so, who would struggle?

Honestly, do we really want any of these conditions? I am sure we do not. These differences are a part of normal living. They give to life the zest of struggle and the rewards of ambition. No great person ever got to fame because life treated him with fairness and equality. True greatness comes at the cost of a life well lived in the presence of unfairness.

Graciousness is a power word. It sounds soft, but it is far from it. It has power to do what hard words and physical struggle against something or some one can never do. The world needs a greater supply of graciousness. It is the quiet word, the firm but pleasant face, in the presence of hostilities and rudeness.

Henry Ward Beecher said, "God appoints our graces to be nurses to other men's weaknesses." That is such an effective way of explaining it. In other words, the gracious people keep our world in balance. They offset the ugly and the mean. Gracious people make us ashamed of our angry outbursts, and are reservoirs of great strength into which others may dip.

The gracious person is the one who takes the dirty end of the stick and cleans it up before handing it to another.

No one ever lived a great life or accomplished any great thing who did not give more of self and time and energy than was expected, more than he was paid for. It is this little bit extra that spells the difference between a life that just gets by and a life that leaves the world a little richer, a little better, and a little happier than when that person came in to it.

This is what Jesus had in mind when he said, "If any man asks you to go with him one mile, go two," and, "If any man asks for your cloak, give him your coat also." He was not talking about extra miles or coats, but about the little bit more than is asked or expected by way of service to others. The big word in life is *give*. With this attitude and approach to life, the getting will automatically take care of itself. If you will give your best of body, mind, and spirit, you will never fail and stay down. You will rise again and eventually will win. It is the way life was created.

It would be quite an experience for us all if we would promise ourselves to live for just twenty-four hours without doing a wrong thing, without saying a mean or untrue word, and without thinking an unclean or belittling thought.

I am sure none of us could accomplish that goal. But what a day it would be to try. It would be a great revelation of ourselves to ourselves. It would show us how easily we slip into gray living, how much time we spend in unworthy living. In short, it probably would make us a bit ashamed.

Just the attempt to live so, no matter how we might fail, would give us the vision of a larger and better world.

Not infrequently we hear some person say, "What I do with my life is nobody's business but mine." I presume most of us have said that at one time or another. But at no time in life is this ever the truth. What every person does with his life is the business of every other person on earth. Sir James Jeans, English mathematician and philosopher, said, "Not a leaf falls but that the whole universe is disturbed." So, in some way whatever I do or say changes the whole world—strengthens it, weakens it, beautifies or mars it.

Small-minded or self-centered people will not accept this. They want to be free of responsibility for any one else's life or happiness. Their own is all they are interested in. And this is the base cause of most unhappiness. No one has the right to live as though his life is his own business and no one else's.

I think the one sentence that has done most to spur me on in life and to set my goals a bit higher was written by Abraham Lincoln. He said, "I will prepare and make ready and someday my chance will come." And his chance did come, but it was no accident or piece of luck or "the breaks" that gave Lincoln his chance. It was his determination to do what he could, where he was, with what he had, to see and accept the responsibilities and the opportunities that would present themselves.

All of us have heard or maybe said, "Boy, if I only had a chance, I'd do great things." I believe the so-called chance is always there before each one of us. And as we prepare ourselves by study and practice toward any worthwhile service, the chance always comes into view. It is a dependable life system. Believe in it. Obey it. And win.

"I will prepare and make ready and some day my chance will come."

What to do with a bad day! Everybody has bad days, days when nothing goes right and everything goes wrong. When one of these days comes your way, don't think you have been singled out by the gods who have it in for you. It is just your turn to have a bad day. And while you are having yours, a few million others will be having their bad days, too. No one has a corner on them, and in the final count it probably is true that everyone winds up with about the same number of them in a lifetime.

However, there are a few rules for the bad days. (1) Keep from speaking any more than is absolutely necessary. On these days it is easy to contract foot-in-mouth disease. (2) Don't make any vital decisions. (3) Force a smile on your face, even if it hurts to do so. (4) Know that the bad day will end and that there will be many more good ones coming up.

It is also good to remember that if it were not for the occasional bad day, the good ones would become very monotonous. The bad days are good testing times to see if our happiness is real enough to carry over and to hold us up until the sun shines again.

When you are deciding on a life's vocation, don't stop with one. Choose two. You were created with the capacity to earn your living with one part of you and to do something wonderful with the other part. Sometimes these can be one and the same, but that is unusual. Most of us do the work necessary to keep us alive and neglect the other areas where we are talented. Many who work in offices, do selling jobs, run machines, or do housework during the day, have the extra capacity to be great volunteer workers. There are stockbrokers who could start a class in money and investing. I know a banker who developed a church orchestra and helped young people who couldn't afford private lessons.

What are you doing with your other talents? Just letting them go to seed? Don't do it. Somebody needs what your other self has to offer. And you will feel more like a complete person if you give it.

Prayer is the longest tool in the universe. With the hands a person can reach just so far. With the eyes and ears he can see and hear just so far. Even with the mind he is limited to that which lies within the reason. But the tool of prayer can reach beyond these limits of physical and mental powers.

We walk the earth boxed within our own limitations. But with the tool of prayer we can poke holes in those limiting walls and ceiling and create a whole new life where beauties, wonders, and even miracles heretofore unknown to us belong and abound.

It is good to pray. It is good because in prayer each of us is aware of a directing force both outside and within, and it gives us confidence.

In prayer we are aware of our connection with a source of never-failing strength, and that gives us a feeling of security. In prayer we are aware of a purpose for our lives, and that gives us a lift of spirit and the desire to go on. In prayer we are aware of a constant Presence, and that takes all fear away because we know we are not alone.

I make this assertion. No normal person is ever at any time without opportunities to do or to be something more than he is. All life is strewn with opportunities that like seeds take root, grow, and produce.

But here is a caution. Though each day has its own opportunities, those of today if neglected could very well never appear again. And many of tomorrow's opportunities will be there only as and if we accept and use those before us today. It is good to assume that today's opportunities will not wait until tomorrow.

At birth you were given certain abilities. At the proper time certain opportunities will appear that will fit those abilities. If you accept them and do your best with them, still greater opportunities will appear. This may be likened to a ladder set up in a dense fog. You can see only one rung at a time. But if you step up on the rung you can see, the next one will come into view.

Make each day an expedition in search for the opportunities that belong to that day and that are especially designed for your abilities. I guarantee that they will appear, and if you grasp and follow them, your future success is assured. New and greater opportunities come only to those who accept those at hand.

Hope is the belief we have in our dreams plus the courage to work toward their fulfillment. Without this belief and without this courage our hopes will remain only dreams, and as such our hopes become but pacifiers lulling us into a false sense of security. Hope is really the other half of our dreams. It is the working half.

And hope is that quality in us that acts as a telescope to look through and beyond our troubles to some good end. It does not eliminate the troubles, but it does cast a light through and beyond them to give us courage to fight on.

One of the facets of hope is patience. It is that which gives us waiting strength, when to wait is a must. It takes knowledge to look at a leaden sky and to believe there is a brilliant sun behind it. But it takes patience to wait for that sun to break through.

Paul wrote, "He that plows ought to plow in hope."

What about our faith? We were all born with the capacity and the need for it. The problem is not whether we have faith, but in what we place it. Frequently all of us misplace our faith. We put it in something or somebody that cannot produce.

We put our faith in our own strength, and then we fall sick. We put our faith in our money and then watch it disappear because of some bad investment or inflation over which we have no control. We put our faith in our business only to wake up some morning and find that a new product or competition has closed our doors.

Faith has to be in something more powerful than ourselves, our possessions, or our businesses. It has to be in a Supreme Being who cares enough and who has power enough to guide us through life even when the going gets rough, to offer what extra strength we need for any catastrophe. In other words our faith must be in a sure thing. And there is nothing that has that quality but the all-powerful love of God.

You have heard that life is a serious business. I'd like to rephrase that. Life is a glorious business that has its serious times. Getting a job is serious business, but how great it is that we are equipped by talent and education to have something to offer. And how wonderful it is that we have so many choices of fields of labor. And though a 5 percent unemployment rate is worrisome, what a spirit lifter it is to know that we have a 95 percent chance of being employed.

Yes, life is serious business, but I would challenge any person to prove that he has more reasons to be depressed than to be elated. This is where the strength of youth lies, in a bouyant spirit, in ability to face a disappointment and to bounce back.

The happiness or unhappiness of life is controlled, not by events, but by which of these we want. Every person sits in control of the elevation of his spirit. Depression will come to all of us because that belongs in life, too, but we determine whether we remain in a depressed state or rise up out of it.

I am convinced that we are what we determine to be. People are not happy because they have no pains, no difficulties, no failures. They are happy because that is what they choose to be.

Be very careful how you handle the reputation of another. Each of us has it in his power to destroy another just by a handful of words. This is why gossip is such a dangerous thing. We can with a few well-timed side remarks do irreparable damage to somebody's life.

All of us have a hard enough struggle in this life trying to get up and get on without having somebody on the sidelines throwing malicious bricks doing damage that can't be repaired. We control what we say about another, but after it is said we have no chance to recall the words.

A father tried to impress upon his son the seriousness of gossip. He had him toss a handful of feathers into the air. Then he told him to pick them all up. The boy said, "I can't, the wind has scattered them every which way." The father answered, "Always remember that before you let out a mouthful of words that discredit another. You can never gather them up again."

You may not have ten cents to your name. Maybe no one ever heard of you. But there is one thing you've got that no one can ever take away from you. You've got ideas. These are among the great gifts of God and very high on the list. He gave to each of us the power to develop ideas that would make a difference to those about us, and maybe to the whole world.

Most people fail, not because of events or competition, but because they gave up digging out and creating new ideas. It may be only a better mousetrap that costs a few cents, but that better mousetrap put thousands to work and made the world a little better for everyone.

Somewhere in each of us is a new song, a new poem, a picture, a better way to clean a house or to make apple butter, a story never told before, maybe one of great courage or faith. I am convinced that when abilities to create were passed out, no one was omitted.

This is what makes life good. It is the giving back to the world whatever good thing we can develop out of the ideas of which our minds are capable.

I have noticed this about genuinely happy people. They are kind. The little thoughtful acts or words that most of us are just too busy or too preoccupied with ourselves and our own needs to practice are sure signs of a happy person. I have never known this test to fail. The normally and continually kind person is a happy person.

So, let us consider the question, each for himself. Am I a kind person? Do I say things that hurt? Am I sarcastic? Do I ever pay attention to or spend time considering the feelings of others? Do I care?

I have known only two people in all my life that I could not get along with. Both of them were basically unhappy people with sharp sarcastic tongues, and both of them went to great pains to honey up to those who might be profitable to them. Their kindness ended there.

Love is a word no one can define. But we may be sure that one of the characteristics that belongs to love is kindness. So, if kindness is a necessary ingredient in both happiness and love, bear down hard on it.

One of the great contributions of the Christian faith is a joyful philosophy of life. It teaches us to look upon life as a great adventure, as a time in which to enjoy the beauty of earth, a time to enjoy friends and things and opportunities, a time to enjoy our work whatever it might be.

Pleasure does belong to our work-a-day world. We must spend so much time at it each day that if we find no joy in our work, we are either in the wrong business, or we have the wrong attitude toward it. So, if we are not enjoying life, let us examine ourselves. Is it because our work is irksome, or would we be unhappy no matter what we were doing? Some people are that way. They are prone to unhappiness. And if you are one of these, for your own sake and for the sake of those about you, I strongly suggest that you see your minister or a counselor because you need not be that way.

We all have differing abilities and talents. But there is one ability that should be common to all. It is the ability to make the sun shine brighter in the dark corners where we live.

No two powers can do more for you than these, belief and fearlessness. We do not fail in this life because we do not have enough ability. Those who fail and stay down do so either because their belief is too small or their fear is too great. These two, belief and fearlessness, may be likened to the side rails of a ladder, something to hold on to while we climb.

I take this thought from a man whom I admire tremendously, Jesus Christ. Those who think him to be a namby-pamby, soft-spoken, weak-kneed man better take another look. He walked the earth without fear of anything or anybody. Much of his life was spent helping others straighten out troubles or to overcome weaknesses. That man had a great dream. Even his friends thought he was not too practical. But with a powerful belief he walked toward that dream and, though it took his life, he made it come true. He gave to the world a code by which men could set their goals higher than the moon and reach them. He made this promise, "And nothing shall be impossible for you." And those who put their backs of belief into it have never been disappointed.

Take a strong grip on these unbreakable, unshakable handrails, belief and fearlessness, and climb away.

It is normal and right for people to want to be great. And what makes anyone great? Any person who does the best he can with what he has is a great person even if his name is never in history, perhaps not even known outside his own family circle.

Abraham Lincoln was a great man, but how about the friend who loaned him those books that he read by candlelight and who started him on his career as a lawyer? Suppose that man had said, "Go buy your own books"? If he had said that we might never have heard of Abraham Lincoln. What that man did —little as it seems to be—was all he had to do in the scheme of things. But because he did that little, the whole course of history was changed.

Don't wait for the big, the glamorous, opportunity to come along. It may not. But do the little things that come to hand each day, and the greatness of life will take care of itself.

Make a place in your life for failure. Many people miss success in this life, but no one misses failure. And if that is so, then we ought to look at failure, know what it is, and decide what we are going to do about it. No one should be proud of his failures, but we can be proud of how we handle them. This is one of the important reasons why some people succeed and others do not. The difference lies in our attitude toward and our understanding of failure and its place in life.

Our failures are our testing grounds. Every great person has come up by way of failures and mistakes recognized as such and has struggled against their repetition. No one leads a charmed life. We are going to stub our toes and bark our shins. My father use to say, "Everyone has to have his own shins kicked to recognize the thin-skinnedness thereof."

Successful people are those who refuse to be thrown by their mistakes, their failures, their sins. They are big enough in mind and spirit to confess them to themselves and to their Maker and to determine that they shall not be repeated.

We can't stop our minds. They were created for perpetual motion. We have to be thinking about something. Psychiatrists tell us that even in our sleep our minds are in action, though at a slower pace. We can't stop thinking any more than we can stop breathing. However, if we don't like the air we are breathing, we can either change the air or go where it is better. In the same manner if our thinking habits are not good, we have to do something to change them. We have to be the boss of our own minds, and many people aren't. You have heard people say, "I can't help it, I just can't get my mind off it." That is an indication that we had better take ourselves in hand and force our minds to do our bidding. The Bible says, "As a man thinks so is he."

If you find yourself thinking wrong thoughts, or worry thoughts, remember that they are doing you great damage, and the quicker you tear your mind off of them the better. And then put your mind to work on something positive. If you don't, the bad ones will return. And anyone can think good and constructive thoughts if he is the boss of his own mind. Are you?

I have said that the two powers that can do the most for you are belief and fearlessness. Now I want to add two more to make up what I call the big four—thankfulness and enjoyment.

An absolute must is a deep sense of appreciation. Some years ago I knew a blind lady whose spirits were bouncy. A man asked her what she had to be happy about. She answered, "I'm alive."

Starting with that, begin to count your blessings. It is one of the greatest exercises for sick dispositions. No one can spend five minutes doing that without pushing the emotional elevator button for "up." And that leads right into the roof garden of enjoying life.

A young girl told me she was afraid to be happy because every time she allowed it something happened to knock her down. I suggested that she turn it around and say that every time she got knocked down something always happened to pick her up again. It does work both ways. It depends on which way you want it.

Life was constructed to produce more happiness than unhappiness. Both belong, but I would put the ratio at ninety-five to five. Here, then, are the four great life-lifters that will hold you steady in the high winds and expose the next rung up: belief, fearlessness, thankfulness, and enjoyment.

I t is easy to pray for those we love or even for those far away, but what about this business of praying for our enemies, for those whom we just don't like, for those who don't like us? Doesn't prayer for these fly in the face of human nature?

Yes, it does. But then, human nature needs to be filed and trimmed and reshaped. Human nature can be pretty ugly.

Praying for those we don't like is good because: (1) It prepares the way for a better relationship with them, (2) it stretches our own natures, (3) it reminds us that we, too, are not without faults.

The Bible says, "Love your enemies." It takes a great person to do that. But the Creator seemed to think we are capable of being great persons, and he ought to know. He created us that way.

Are you a great person, big in heart and mind? Do you really love your fellows? Here is a good way to find out. Examine yourself on this matter. Do you rejoice with members of your own family or with friends who have received some recognition, who have done well in life, who are the recipients of some good fortune? Does it please you that these honors have come to them? Or do you find yourself responding with jealousy? Do you say things that would belittle the honor?

I believe this to be one of the hardest tests of Christianity. Can we rejoice in another's good fortune when we have lived lives just as good and worked just as hard but did not receive any honors?

Envy is one of the great hurdles of life. It does much damage within families. If you are afflicted with the curse of envy, you had better do some hard praying about that because it is a killer of happiness.

In the musical play "Carousel" the words of a song tell us to walk on with hope in our hearts, and we'll never walk alone. I like that. It gives a reason for our hope. If we have hope in our hearts we will never walk alone because there will be walking beside us all the forces of the universe. It is the hope in our hearts that opens the way for God to walk in with big ideas for us to follow.

William Montford said, "Eternity is the divine treasure house, and hope is the window by means of which mortals are permitted to see the things which God is preparing." That is a good definition of hope. Man sees his God and all the goodness of life only through the window of his hope. And without those windows the light of his life must be a gray one indeed, and his vision is limited to the small area of his physical sight.

For what are you hoping? Is it big enough to be worthy of giving your life to its fulfilling? If it isn't, you need a bigger hope. Yours is too small.

A sure cause of fatigue is brooding. It is hard enough and penalty enough to have to take losses in life and to pay for our mistakes, but to brood over them is to take the losses and pay the price over and over again. This isn't fair. It is overcharging ourselves. It is piling weights upon us that we were never meant to carry.

To brood over our losses or mistakes is to invite sickness. Our bodies are made so they will respond to the dictates of our minds. So, if the mind creates a low spiritual ebb, pretty soon the tone of the body will begin to sag. And in the same manner, if the mind seeks a high level on which to promenade, the body will respond with an upward surge of strength and well-being.

Everyone has a pool of reserve strength that can be released just by lifting up the thoughts. We will be better physically, and much happier, if we will take our minds off the brooding level and put them on the mountain top of great thoughts. To a very great extent every person controls his own health.

This is a provable truth. The happy life must always have religion in it if it is to hold together when the going gets tough. Anyone can be lighthearted and gay when the sun shines and all is well. Lightheartedness and gaiety are surface responses. But happiness, girded with faith, is still there holding the spirits from going to pieces when the sun does not shine and when everything is not all right. And for this deep sense of adequacy to meet whatever comes in life, there must be a well-grounded faith in a Supreme Being to whom we can look for a steadying hand and additional strength. No one has enough strength, courage, and wisdom to meet all life's problems and responsibilities alone and still walk on straight up. To do our best we have to have help and guidance from a higher source. And being in touch with that Higher Source is what we call religion.

But this must be remembered. That faith, that religion, could very well increase our difficulties and add to our trials because those who believe attempt more and stick their necks out farther. And this is why those who are deeply committed in faith can accomplish the unbelievable. They, knowing God is with them, dare to try for greater goals.

There is a great deal of nonsense these days about people who can't help what they are and what they do because of what their parents were.

There is no question that heredity leaves its mark on all of us and so does the environment into which we are born and forced to live until we are able to shift for ourselves. But if these were the controlling factors in what we become then none of us would be responsible for our actions, and by the same token none of us could take credit for the good things we do or the successes we build. We would never agree to this. We want credit for our efforts.

So let's quit hiding behind our heredity or our environment when we fail or when we do things we ought not do. Each of us is born with a will that is stronger than either heredity or environment. Therefore, each one of us is responsible for what he is and for what he does. If we want any credit for any good things we do or any honorable achievements, we must also be prepared to take the responsibility for our failures and our misdeeds.

We usually think of prayer as a person talking to God. And that is true of course. But full, useful, effective prayer includes talking to one's own inner self. It is this inner self that was created in the image of God. It is the finest, highest, most perfect self. Prayer to God without the recognition of one's inner self isn't of much value because when God answers prayer, he does not by some magic make the thing or condition we prayed for appear. But in his answer he opens the way for us to do the accomplishing. And to do this God works through the inner self, which is the perfect self. This is where a person sits down and thinks his highest thoughts and comes to his deepest convictions.

Everyone has a dual personality, the outer self that meets and does business with the outside world and the inner self which is the true and eternal person. Full prayer consists of speaking to God, listening to God, and conferring with one's own inner self. Each person has a special place on this earth and a special reason for being here. He can find that place and that reason only by opening the inner self to God.

It was William Shakespeare who told us that all the world is a stage and that all the people on it are players. How very true it is, and how picturesque the thought. The world is our stage and you and I have been chosen to play some part in the unfolding drama of life. Maybe at the moment, the stage you find yourself on is a very poor one, and maybe the part you are asked to play doesn't offer the opportunity for the best that is in you. Maybe you know you are worthy of a better, a more important part. And maybe you are. But don't quit. Don't walk out on the play. Whatever part you are asked to fill, fill it with the best you've got. You see, always there are talent scouts standing in the wings watching. The world needs those who play the small parts, for usually it is to those who play them well that the larger more important parts are given.

It is just common sense. If you don't play the small parts well, who would choose you for the big parts? Wherever you are, whatever your part is, play it like a veteran, because on that stage you are being trained for the bigger parts. Here is our guarantee. If we do the best we can with the opportunities that are ours, bigger and better ones will be offered.

Friends—how much we need them and how much they need us. A very good friend of mine said to me, "Any one is lucky if in his entire lifetime he has found five friends who would stick with him through thick and thin, through failure and success." That is a serious condemnation, isn't it?

How quick we are to criticise even those we call friends. How quick we are to turn away when one has fallen, made a mistake, done a fool thing. But it is at this point that his need for us is at its peak. Are most of us fair-weather friends? It is a good question to ponder.

I believe it is our responsibility on this earth to throw a friendly arm about the shoulders of one who is stumbling and to speak a word that will tell that person that here is a friend. That may be all that is needed to bring him back, to lift his spirits, and to make the sun shine for him.

No one is enough in himself. That is why the commandment, "Love your neighbor as yourself." And that means be a friend especially when others are turning away. You might just save a life. It has been known to happen just that way.

Some people don't like to make decisions. They don't want the responsibility if something goes wrong. They are afraid of failure. Here I believe is the dividing line between successful and unsuccessful people. The willingness to take on the obligation of decision is a necessity for success.

You will be presented with many opportunities to make decisions. Should you stand for what you know to be right, or should you go along with the crowd? Sometimes it is costly to make the right decision, sometimes it is a lonesome business, sometimes it hurts. But here is where great lives are made. And here is where those who refuse to pay the price of right decisions begin their trip into unsuccessful or at best mediocre living.

A few brave decisions made early in life will oil the hinges of the doors of opportunity.

We hear so much about making one's mark in the world. Perhaps we should speak of making one's mark *on* the world. That I believe is the reason every one of us is on this earth, to make some special mark on the world, a mark that no one else is designed to make.

This ought to make us feel good and very important. Yes, it is right and good that we should feel important. In fact, if we are going to make our mark on the world, we must feel important enough to do it.

But how do we know what mark we are to make on the world? That is one of the greatest and finest mysteries of life, that each one of us is guided to the place and the opportunity to do that for which he was created. It doesn't take more than a casual look at our world to know that it was not put together with guesswork and maybes. It is a perfectly planned and organized world in which we are especially created to fit. And if we obey the laws of God and seek his guidance, the steps we are to take will be shown to us—one step at a time.

Everybody has his own pet ideas about what this world needs, from a better ten-cent cigar to a new system of government.

So, I have mine. It is this. We have too many people living way beneath their abilities and capacities. We have too many people doing fair or pretty good work, too many people satisfied just to get by, not too good not too bad, just average.

Once I told an older woman for whom I had much respect that I hoped to do a good enough job in a certain field. She struck her fist on the desk and cried, "Harold Drown, good enough is not good enough." I have thought of that so many times. Good enough is not good enough.

What the world needs is more men and women to say, "I can do better than that. I can live a better life. I can create something more worthy of my ability."

The world needs men and women to believe that they are honored by God in being given the right and the ability to manage life and to do something with it that would be a credit to themselves, to their fellows, and to God.

One night I heard a philosopher on TV say, "Life is like a book with chapters in it." But this is not a true picture of life. When a book has been printed, no one can change a chapter, add one, or take one out, not even the author. However, in life there is always a new chapter to be written, and each of us may write whatever he wishes in that new chapter.

No matter how bad the latest chapter in the book of life may be, we can add a new chapter. And if the new chapter is well-lived, it can take the cutting edge off the unhappy chapter, the unclean chapter.

At the close of a day God mercifully draws the shade of night. In a few hours he turns the page recording that day over and gives us a fresh sheet, a new day, on which we are invited to write a new chapter, a happy one, a clean one, one to be proud of.

Would you like to know what the future holds for you? I think everyone would like to peek into tomorrow. And it is possible. How? Just draw a word picture of the kind of person you want to be twenty-five years from now. Then don't just wish for it but tear into it with your whole life. And, presto-chango, twenty-five years later you've got it. How do I know? The Bible says so. "Whatsoever you sow that shall you also reap." And that works for bad seeds as well as good. So, just choose your seeds and predict your own future.

What freedoms we have! Even to choose whether we shall live good lives or bad, successful or failing. But we are assured that whichever we choose and bend our efforts to, we will get. What a thought! Sow good things and reap more of them. I like that.

A young man in his thirties decided he wanted to be a C.P.A. He went back to college. He is now a very successful C.P.A. in New York city. Whatever you sow, that you shall reap. That works just as surely as the sun rises in the east and sets in the west. A neighbor of mine planted cottonwood trees to get quick shade. He got it. He also got a troublesome root system and a dirty fall of fluff.

In this world everything reaps its own harvest. That makes it a dependable world. Corn must come from corn and beans from beans. So, choose your seeds. Sow them and reap them.

No one should ever stop learning. No one should ever stop reaching for more knowledge. You wouldn't willingly wear a twenty-year-old, out-of-fashion overcoat, but many people are walking around with minds that stopped reaching for knowledge years ago.

The world is filled with secrets, wonderful secrets of power and beauty undreamed of. And it is our privilege to find those secrets and to release them to the world. This is what learning is for. Each person is born to discover some small part of the secrets of life, and insofar as we neglect our opportunities, we cheat the whole world out of that which we could have contributed.

I am personally convinced that if you will keep on struggling to improve your mind and to use what you discover for the happiness and the welfare of others, you will never need to worry about your place in life. It will be a good one and a happy one.

One of the ancients said, "Live for something. Do good and leave behind you a monument of virtue that the storms of time can never destroy."

We can all live at peace within ourselves no matter what troubles may be raging outside if only we have the satisfaction of knowing that we have done the best we could with what we were given, that we have done no man harm, and that we have helped someone else along the way.

Happy is that person to whom others like to come with their joys and their sorrows, with their too-heavy loads and their successes. But this position of honor is built over many years out of little kindnesses and words of comfort and encouragement. This is something worth living for. And while we are so living in helpfulness to others, we are building houses for ourselves to live in, houses of memories that are pleasant to recall.

Life is like a candle. When a candle is lighted it throws off light for others to see as well as for the one who lighted it. Light is something we can't keep all to ourselves. It won't shine for us alone. However, in giving off its light to others, the candle uses itself up. It burns itself out. If, on the other hand, it had never been lighted, it would always retain its full size. It would never burn out. But whoever notices an unlighted candle?

Life is like that. We can use ourselves up by spending ourselves in the service of others, making their pathway a little brighter. Or we can do nothing for others, just preserve ourselves. And maybe we will live a little longer that way. Maybe we will have more for ourselves that way. But, like the unlighted candle, no one will ever notice us, for there is no light around us.

There are three kinds of people in the world. There are those who thrill to nothing. They walk about with sullen, set, or angry faces. None of us likes to be with them. They make life taste sour. Then there are people who thrill only to the accumulation of things, to the swelled bank accounts, the overflowing safety deposit boxes. These people never care much about others and are not responsive to the needs of the less fortunate. But then there are those who thrill just to be alive, to be in the company of others, to do their bit along the highway of helpfulness. These are the ones who, with their gracious manner and the pleasant faces, attract and have the chance to help those who find life difficult —the troubled, the fallen, the weak. These are the people who are truly building the kingdom of God. They know and are living the words from the Bible, "What does the Lord require of you but to do justice, and to love kindness, and to walk humbly with your God?"

Every age has its own idiomatic phrases. One that is popular today is, You've got it made. I like that one, providing the ifs of life are recognized and made a part of the phrase.

You've got it made IF you prepare yourself by getting all you can out of your educational opportunities.

You've got it made IF you try your best to discover your talents and then are willing to work, not forty hours a week, but as many hours as it takes to develop those talents.

You've got it made IF you are not afraid of failure, IF you walk confident of success, and IF you face life with a glad-to-be-alive spirit.

And finally you've got it made IF you have an unshakable belief in the constant presence of God with whom you are on good terms and with whom you talk frequently about your plans, your needs, and your hopes.